Sacraments

THE PRESENCE
OF GRACE

Bernard Häring, C.Ss.R.

LIGUORI CELEBRATION SERIES

Liguori
ONE LIGUORI DRIVE
LIGUORI MO 63057-9999

Imprimi Potest:
Richard Thibodeau, C.Ss.R.
Provincial, Denver Province
The Redemptorists

Imprimatur:
Most Reverend Michael J. Sheridan
Auxiliary Bishop, Archdiocese of St. Louis

ISBN 0-7648-0531-2
Library of Congress Catalog Card Number: 99-64299

© 1999, Munich Province of the Redemptorists
Printed in the United States of America
03 02 01 00 99   5 4 3 2 1

Scripture quotations from the *New Revised Standard Version of the Bible,* © 1989 by the Division of Christian Education of the National Council of the Churches of Christ in the USA. Used with permission. All rights reserved.

Quotations from Vatican II documents taken from *Vatican Council II, the basic sixteen documents: Constitutions, Decrees, Declarations. A completely revised translation in inclusive language.* Austin Flannery, OP, general editor. © 1996 Costello Publishing Company: Northport, NY and Dominican Publications: Dublin, Ireland. "My Confession of Faith" excerpts edited from a series in *The Tablet* (July 28, August 4, 1990).

These reflections have been revised and compiled from the following original sources: *Prayer: The Integration of Faith and Life,* © 1975, Notre Dame, IN: Fides Publishers. *The Sacraments and Your Everyday Life,* © 1976, Liguori, MO: Liguori Publications. *In Pursuit of Wholeness: Healing in Today's Church,* © 1985, Liguori, MO: Liguori Publications.

Cover design by Wendy Barnes

Table *of* Contents

Part One

Signs
of
Grace

The Primacy *of* Grace

Grace *(charis)* means the graciousness of God in turning the divine countenance to us. It is a sign of God's nearness, a word of love which arouses in us an answering love. Grace means gentleness, the attractive energy of true love; it means alliance, a reciprocal relationship which, however, remains wholly the gift of God. On our part, it is received with the awareness that it is an undeserved gift, and this awareness energizes us, teaches us, disciplines us, gives orientation to our whole life.

The sacraments are divine signs that provoke human initiatives of authentic love, of true mercy, and of new dimensions in personal relationships. As long as we continue to speak of the sacraments and of grace in a language of causality, we fail in two respects. First, we neglect the human hunger for personal meaning, for more humane and intimate relationships; and second, we fail to stress grace, the divine initiative that encourages human openness, spontaneity, and initiative.

The scholastic doctrine expresses the primacy of grace in the sacraments by the phrase *opus operatum:* The sacrament is the work of God. But the work of God always has the character of Word, of message. When we speak of *opus operatum,* therefore, we speak of the Word in whom all things are created, and of the new creation in the Word Incarnate who, by all that he does, speaks to our minds and hearts.

We are unworthy of God's grace. The sacramental economy continually reminds us that it is only because we are redeemed—through Christ's passion, death, and Resurrection—that we have access to God; only because we are redeemed do we receive the signs of God's graciousness and goodness. The sacraments, precisely because they make us aware of the gratuitousness of redemption, transform us and constitute us as signs of the reign of God.

A full understanding of the sacraments teaches us to accept all things with a spirit of gratitude for the goodness of God. Through the sacraments, Christ continually reminds us: *"You did not choose me but I chose you. And I appointed you to go and bear fruit, fruit that will last, so that the Father will give you whatever you ask him in my name"* (John 15:16).

When we become fully conscious of being redeemed and elected by divine mercy, then we bear the fruits of mercy, of goodness, of thanksgiving. The farewell discourses teach this sacramental reality, which is continued in the Church:

> *"I am the true vine, and my Father is the vinegrower. He removes every branch in me that bears no fruit. Every branch that bears fruit he prunes to make it bear more fruit. You have already been cleansed by the word that I have spoken to you. Abide in me as I abide in you. Just as the branch cannot bear fruit by itself unless it abides in the vine, neither can you unless you abide in me. I am the vine, you are the branches. Those who abide in me and I in them bear much fruit, because apart from me you can do nothing."*
>
> John 15:1-4

Authentic catechesis, and the sacramental celebration itself, transform us precisely because they make us all the more conscious that:

"[God] destined us for adoption as his children through Jesus Christ, according to the good pleasure of his will, to the praise of his glorious grace that he freely bestowed on us in the Beloved. In him we have redemption through his blood, the forgiveness of our trespasses, according to the riches of his grace that he lavished on us. With all wisdom and insight he has made known to us the mystery of his will, according to his good pleasure that he set forth in Christ, as a plan for the fullness of time, to gather up all things in him, things in heaven and things on earth."

Ephesians 1:5-10

GRACED SACRAMENTS

When the sacraments are promoted as an added set of "duties," over and beyond those imposed by the Ten Commandments and by a codified "natural law," we commit a grave error. The sacraments are gifts, gratuities of Christ's love, efficacious signs of salvation through which dignity, grace, and commitment to a Christian life come to us. They cannot be understood in the abstract, or as bare precepts. Christ is the Word Incarnate, flesh and blood, fully visible and attractive. So must the Christian message that is presented to those who wish to follow him be.

The proper place and task of sacraments is to show, in a human way, the expanse and primacy of God's love and the loving response we are expected to give. Sacraments bring a visible and fascinating presence of God's love in Christ Jesus, which manifests itself in the Church and its members through the work of the Holy Spirit. In looking at sacraments, therefore, we always hold the following premises in mind:

- Even in speaking of the seven sacraments, the point of view remains always the *unique sacramentality of Christ,* the Word Incarnate. Sacraments are but signs of his presence among us, symbols of his benevolence. The sacraments will be considered in their capacity to open us to a broader view of the saving presence of Christ in history and in the daily events of our lives and of our times.

- The sacraments are *privileged and efficacious signs of grace.* They are true symbols of God's gracious presence, instituted by Christ and dispensed by the Church in obedience to him. This does not mean, however, that the sacraments hold a monopoly on grace. The fact that Christ has given us these special signs, these invitations to grace, does not mean that he—or the Holy Spirit—is unable or unwilling to convey salvation in other ways. The opposite is true. As privileged signs of salvation, the sacraments open us and direct our attention to all the other ways in which God shows graciousness. They demand vigilance to the signs of the times, and great respect and reverence for the wonderful ways in which God works and is manifested outside of the sacramental life of the Church.

- It may not be easy to find the happy medium which, on the one hand, considers the sacraments of the Church as the *privileged key* which provides an understanding of the economy of salvation and, on the other hand, does not assert a monopoly of the sacraments on God's grace. However, a theology of the world, centered on the sacramental character of creation in the light of redemption, grasps the dynamics and vitality of the seven sacraments. This broader vision of sacramentality also overcomes tendencies toward mere ritualism.

- We remember that for many centuries the Church stood as the sacrament of salvation, and the Church celebrated the sacraments without exactly determining their number. In the sacramental theology of past centuries, an overemphasis on the role of the minister, and great stress on ritual and rubrics, resulted in underdevelopment of the doctrine of the *universal priesthood of the people*. Today, much more attention is given to the active participation of the faithful.

- In speaking of the sacraments, and of a sacramental vision of life, we must be mindful of the modern phenomena of secularization and desacralization. Past overemphasis on stones, places, and other "sacred things" concealed, to a considerable extent, the real sacramental message. Desacralization, then, can generate a more authentic concentration on the sacraments, and a deeper, more serious understanding of their sanctifying effect. Accepting the challenge of secularization, we will not stress ritual and rubrics; rather, we will question the efficacy of the sign. Does the sacrament really become a *visible sign*? Does it truly communicate the inviting and challenging Good News of God's love and mercy and faithfulness?

• We still have to place in a sacramental perspective the problem of the salvation of all peoples. Wherever and whenever God gives signs of love and mercy, with the grace of the Holy Spirit and in view of the salvation prepared in Christ, these signs can generate a living faith in the One who is the source of salvation. All the signs of mercy, of goodness, of solidarity— which quicken human life—can have a *sacramental character* insofar as there is discernible in them the dynamic presence of Christ. In saying this, however, let us not forget the privileged role of the sacramental signs instituted by Christ and entrusted to the Church.

CHRIST'S COMING IN BAPTISM

"...and the Holy Spirit descended upon him in bodily form like a dove. And a voice came from heaven, 'You are my Son, the Beloved; with you I am well pleased' " (Luke 3:22).

When Jesus was baptized in the Jordan, his meeting with all the others who were baptized at the same time was very important. He joined them in a wonderful solidarity—the person for others, the person for all people.

To those who know that they are sinners—who are baptized in the hope of and readiness for conversion—the coming of Christ becomes an epiphany: a revelation of the Holy Spirit, and of the love of the Father for his Son who is ready to bear the burden of all humankind.

When he comes into our life, the Father's love for him—and for us—becomes visible. On the cross, when Jesus is baptized again in his own blood—the blood of the Covenant—he is near to all of us, praying for those who have crucified him and welcoming into his reign the thief at his side.

By our baptism, we partake in the baptism of Christ. He himself baptizes us, through the Spirit, calling us into the Covenant sealed by his blood. Christ meets the baptized, wanting to abide with us, and to transform us into mirror images of his own solidarity and all-embracing love. When we have learned to make our decisions and to orient our lives around prayer—"What can I give to the Lord for what he has given me?"—the happy awareness that Christ is with us in our daily lives becomes more and more intense.

But it is not just at the moment of the reception of the

SPIRITUAL PILGRIMAGE
WITH
HIS HOLINESS POPE BENEDICT XVI
ON HIS PASTORAL VISIT TO TURKEY
NOV. 28 – DEC. 1, 2006

Heavenly Father, from whom every family in heaven and on earth takes its name, we humbly ask that you sustain, inspire, and protect your servant, Pope Benedict XVI, as he goes on pilgrimage to Turkey – a land to which St. Paul brought the Gospel of your Son; a land where once the Mother of your Son, the Seat of Wisdom, dwelt; a land where faith in your Son's true divinity was definitively professed. Bless our Holy Father, who comes as a messenger of truth and love to all people of faith and good will dwelling in this land so rich in history. In the power of the Holy Spirit, may this visit of the Holy Father bring about deeper ties of understanding, cooperation, and peace among Roman Catholics, the Orthodox, and those who profess Islam. May the prayers and events of these historic days greatly contribute both to greater accord among those who worship you, the living and true God, and also to peace in our world so often torn apart by war and sectarian violence.

We also ask, O Heavenly Father, that you watch over and protect Pope Benedict and entrust him to the loving care of Mary, under the title of Our Lady of Fatima, a title cherished both by Catholics and Muslims. Through her prayers and maternal love, may Pope Benedict be kept safe from all harm as he prays, bears witness to the Gospel, and invites all peoples to a dialogue of faith, reason, and love. We make our prayer through Christ, our Lord. Amen.

Prayer composed by Bishop William E. Lori, Supreme Chaplain

KNIGHTS OF COLUMBUS

sacrament that we meet Christ. He comes into our life to be with us and in us, and to awaken our consciousness to the wonder of his abiding presence and to gratitude for it.

To live according to the gifts of these sacraments means to help each other toward greater awareness of his being with us. It is in this perspective that we can understand when, in the language of the charismatic renewal, people speak about baptism in the Holy Spirit. They have not in mind a new sacrament, but through their experience as members of a community of faith, love, and praise, they invite the Spirit so that the sacraments of baptism and confirmation may become a more conscious reality in their lives.

In shared prayer we are aware of our being baptized by the Holy Spirit. If we pray with each other and for each other, that the Spirit may come upon us, and if at the same time we work to build up the reign of God, we are on the way to a full reciprocity of consciousness: we are experiencing more intimately the presence of Christ, who has baptized us and continues to baptize us in the Holy Spirit. We open ourselves to him so that, with him, we can praise the Father and bear fruit in love for the life of the world.

INFANT BAPTISM

Normally, the celebration of the sacrament of baptism ought to be a community celebration of the people of God for the praise of the glory of God's grace. It should be a celebration of the Covenant, and of the active belonging to it which sustains the faith of all its members. It ought also to express the renewed commitment of all the faithful to the vocation which they received in their own baptism, and of their pledge to be an effective community of faith for the infants to be baptized.

The communal celebration of the baptism of infants ought to be recognized as a privileged sign of grace and of justification by grace, without asserting, however, that it is the exclusive way of salvation. Praise for the sacramental sign of grace ought not to diminish praise for God's will to save all, and for Christ who wanted to die for all. The assurance of salvation which the sacramental sign gives ought to be appreciated, but not in a way that would cast doubt on the universality of God's salvific will and work.

A child's baptism ought never to be considered as an isolated moment, but rather as an intense and privileged moment in a whole series of developments, during which the baptized gradually receives and responds to the Good News of God's graciousness. All of education ought to be conceived in the perspective and in the light of baptism, as a postbaptismal catechumenate which makes clear that baptism is the initial point of development— not the point of arrival.

Except in cases of imminent danger of death, there should be firm refusal to baptize infants who are not in any way really inserted into the community of faith. Official church legislation forbids one to be baptized if there is no hope of a postbaptismal catechumenate. Pastoral decisions should make clear that the baptismal celebration expresses the fact and event of a community of faith receiving the neophyte, and guaranteeing that neophyte the necessary future evangelization and its attendant commitment.

The faith of the parents and of the family is a fundamental criterion, but not the only one. If the parents are undependable as heralds of faith, but there is a community of lively faith into which the child can be integrated, it is possible that this community will guarantee the evangelization of the child. The weaker the solidarity of salvation in a community, the less likely will the liturgy be an expression of faith and of praise of God, and the less justified can be the baptism of infants whose parents are not disposed to commit themselves effectively to the child's Christian education.

Prayer

In awareness of the reality of our baptism and in gratitude for it, we praise you, Father, Lord of heaven and earth. We praise you because your servant, Jesus Christ, wanted to be baptized with the crowd of humble people who knew that they were sinners. We thank you that, through baptism, you gather your people, to make them one and holy.

We beg you, Father, to grant to your Church a deeper knowledge of what you mean by baptism: that infants should be baptized not only with water and words, but that they should be truly inserted into a community of believers, thus to experience the joy and strength of faith. Help us to build up that reign in which we can more fully understand what baptism in the Holy Spirit means for us. Send us your Spirit, that our lives may bear the fruits of the Spirit in kindness, gentleness, generosity, spontaneity, and creativity.

Assist our efforts in prayer. Let our prayer, and our lives, bring to the whole Church the message that the Spirit is truly our life and our guide.

Come, Holy Spirit, cleanse us from our sins. Let us share in the joy of the risen Lord, and let our life be joined with him, so that we may always experience his nearness.

THE PRESENCE OF CHRIST IN THE EUCHARIST

The summit of the presence of the risen Lord and the Holy Spirit is the eucharistic celebration. The Eucharist is the great mystery of faith in which Christ speaks to us by giving himself to us as the bread of eternal life. Christ is present, too, in his Word; he himself is the Good News for us. Whenever we are open to the grace of the Holy Spirit in a community of believers, united in Christ who is our hope, and ready to receive his Word and to act on it, we discover anew that Christ's Word is, for us, "spirit and life" (see John 6:63).

The whole eucharistic celebration is a Word and a gift of life that aims at our total conversion, our complete transformation in the Lord. The Eucharist is infinitely more than a memorial of past events; it is the Word Incarnate who reminds us of those past events, which then become a present reality for all believers.

Christ's presence in the Eucharist—through his living Word, and under the species of bread and wine—is not separated into two entities. We distinguish two different aspects, but they are one reality: Christ meeting us, speaking to us here and now, revealing to us the final meaning of all the events of the history of salvation. "The bread of life" gives life to the world, so that the world may live in him, with him, and through him.

The eucharistic presence of Christ is the strongest, the most miraculous, and the most effective presence in this world. When Christ meets us in the power of the Spirit, whom he bestows on us, we can receive this wonderful gift with thanks and praise, and respond by entrusting ourselves wholeheartedly to him, to become his witnesses to the ends of the earth.

Only through the power of the Spirit does the eucharistic celebration become a peak experience in which we reach full reciprocity of consciousness. Through the Spirit, who is the self-giving love between the Father and the Son, we receive—in the Eucharist—a share in the love of the Son for the Father and the Father for the Son. Thus we receive the greatest gift: Christ himself. And we too can give ourselves totally to him and to his mission.

When Christ foretold the Eucharist—*"Those who eat my flesh and drink my blood abide in me, and I in them"* (John 6:56)—many of his disciples demurred and left him. His words made no sense to them. Jesus reminded them, then, of the gift of the Spirit:

> *"Does this offend you? Then what if you were to see the Son of Man ascending to where he was before? It is the spirit that gives life; the flesh is useless. The words that I have spoken to you are spirit and life."*

> John 6:61b-63

It is only through the Holy Spirit that Jesus is the bread of life, available for all, ready to be eaten by all who need him. It is only through the Holy Spirit that we, filled with gratitude for this greatest of gifts, can be ready to abandon ourselves to Christ and to follow him as servants of humanity. Since Christ, by the power of the Holy Spirit, gives nothing less than his life-giving body and blood in order to transform us into faithful people of the Covenant, we can trust that the Spirit also gives us the strength and courage to give nothing less than ourselves for Christ and his reign.

We cannot reach that reciprocity of consciousness with Christ, which is the aim of the Eucharist, unless we share Christ's love with our neighbor, because Christ has shed the blood of the Covenant for all of us. His presence in the Eucharist is infinitely dynamic, a divine energy that builds up and makes indispensable the unity of his disciples. When the Lord encounters us in the Eucharist, he wants to unite every fiber of our lives with himself. It is a communion of life and love. To receive Christ truthfully is to confirm again our readiness to be active and constructive members of his mystical body, the Church. Receiving his body in faith, we become his body.

Prayer

Thank you, Lord, because the memory of your Incarnation, your Passion and Death, your Resurrection and Ascension, is not just an account that comes to us from past history. You yourself come, graciously, to remind us that you were born for us, you have suffered for us, you are alive for us. You want to live in us and with us in order to continue, through us, your saving love for all people in all time. Lord, we believe that you are the life of our life, the strength of our strength, and the road of our salvation.

Thank you, Lord, that our thanksgiving is not ours alone, but that it is united with the thanks and praise you have offered to our heavenly Father. Grant, by the Holy Spirit, that we may always celebrate the memory of your Incarnation, Passion, Death, Resurrection, and Ascension with such great faith, joy, and gratitude; that all our life becomes, in union with you, praise and thanksgiving to the Father. Help us to honor the name of God by being one with your redemptive love for all the world.

THE LORD'S PRESENCE IN THE EFFECTIVE SIGNS OF RECONCILIATION

All who live in union with Christ are asked to be, for each other, signs of reconciliation and helpers in salvation. *"If another member of the church sins against you, go and point out the fault when the two of you are alone. If the member listens to you, you have regained that one"* (Matthew 18:15). Whenever the saving event of familial correction and encouragement occurs, a particularly active presence of Christ is guaranteed.

We honor this reconciling presence in prayer, relying on God's grace:

"Truly I tell you, if two of you agree on earth about anything you ask, it will be done for you by my Father in heaven. For where two or three

are gathered in my name, I am there among them."

Matthew 18:19-20

From its context, this text is evidently related to familial correction by a brother or sister in Christ, as well as to the reconciling effort of the official Church and its ministers.

"If we live by the Spirit, let us also be guided by the Spirit. Let us not become conceited, competing against one another, envying one another. My friends, if anyone is detected in a transgression, you who have received the Spirit should restore such a one in a spirit of gentleness. Take care that you yourselves are not tempted. Bear one another's burdens, and in this way you will fulfill the law of Christ."

Galatians 5:25—6:2

By faith and grace, we recognize the gratuitousness of redemption and the power of the Spirit, and our gratitude moves us to help each other, to strengthen each other, and to bear one another's burdens. Up to the time of Albert the Great and Thomas Aquinas, familial correction, offered in a spirit of gentleness and in awareness that we all depend on God's patience and graciousness, and followed by humble avowal of the fault and by prayer, was considered a kind of sacrament, a *particular expression* of the sacrament of divine forgiveness. This vision did not at all diminish the special role of the priest as a minister of reconciliation. If we experience Christ's gracious presence in our daily lives, helping each other to overcome limitations and faults, then we also come to a better understanding of the celebration of the Church's sacrament of reconciliation.

It is always Christ who comes and assures us of forgiveness, but he has chosen to do it in a very visible and effective way through the ministry of the Church. In the sacrament of reconciliation we meet the priest who, through his charism and mission, is truly a sign of the presence of the Good Shepherd, of the Divine Physician. We see, then, the essence of this sacrament: that it is not so much our own endeavor but, rather, Christ's. Through grace, the mercy of the Father, and his own gentle presence and healing power, Christ calls us to the humble avowal of our sins and the redirection of our life toward his goodness. Through the healing kindness of our neighbor and the consoling message of the commissioned messenger of reconciliation, Christ kindles in us a new courage, and the desire to respond to his call to follow him and to carry out our share in the redemptive mission of the Church.

Prayer

It is right and fitting, a sign of your gracious presence and a way of salvation, to render thanks always and everywhere to you, all-merciful God. When first we fell into sinfulness and alienation, you did not abandon us. As a sign of salvation, you gave to Adam and Eve sons like Abel and Seth, who knew how to invoke your name and to praise your goodness. When Cain slaughtered his brother, you yourself made a sign on his face that slaughter should not go on. And when the earth was flooded with sin, you saved Noah, his family, and all the species of animals out of the chaos of waters.

You made Joseph, whom his brothers had sold into slavery, a wonderful sign of forgiveness and reconciliation. And when your people in slavery called to you for liberation, you led them out of Egypt, through the Red Sea, through the desert, and over the Jordan, into the promised land.

You taught the prostitute, Rahab, to show mercy to the ambassadors of your people, and in turn you taught your people to show mercy to her.

When the anointed king, David, offended you gravely by taking another man's wife and killing her husband, you sent Nathan to shake his conscience and make him aware of his crime.And when he showed repentance, you made known to David your mercy and reconciled him.

At the appointed time you sent Jesus Christ, your Son, and made him the great sacrament of reconciliation, the Good Shepherd who seeks the lost sheep, the Divine Physician who heals the sick, the source of living water who, by the power of the Holy Spirit, can raise to life those who were dead in their sins.

Therefore, with the angels and saints, with all those who, throughout history, have been messengers of your peace and ministers of reconciliation, we commit ourselves to the same

mission: to be signs of your merciful presence,
and thus to praise your name.

THE NEARNESS OF CHRIST TO—AND THROUGH—THE PRIEST

The priest is called to be, above all, a man of prayer. By his mission, he is a hearer of the Word of God; he treasures it up in his heart and ponders it. He has made the main purpose of his life to be an adorer of God in spirit and in truth, and to help all the priestly people of God to abide in the Word of the Lord, to pray, and to find a synthesis between faith and life—to the honor and glory of God.

Since the priest is sent to speak not in his own name but in the name of the Lord—to make known the Lord's loving presence—the first condition for his life's fulfillment is that he should live in the deepest possible union with the One who sends him. Only in this way can he live his special charism, to make known to his brothers and sisters that the Lord is near.

The priest must be rich in the qualities of sympathy and human understanding. To the very best of his ability, he has to acquire a wide-ranging and profound knowledge of humankind and of the world in which he lives.

The relationship of the priest with other believers is by no means a one-way street. It is through the Christian community, through his parents and his friends, that he learns how to pray, how to grow in the knowledge and in the joy of faith. To be a sign of God's loving presence, he needs the love, the kindness, patience, and understanding of those he ministers to.

Prayer

*We pray to you, Christ, our prophetic high priest,
and we thank you, because you inspire men
and women to dedicate themselves wholly to
your Gospel, and to be for us signs of your own
total consecration to the Gospel of our heavenly
Father.*

*Lord Jesus, we thank you for the priestly
ministry that brings us into closer contact with
you. Send your Church priests who are also
prophets, who have experienced your holiness
and your kindness, and are people of faith and
hope from whom we can learn what it means to
adore God in spirit and in truth.*

THE PRESENCE OF CHRIST IN MARRIAGE

God is love, the source of all goodness. Wherever we
find true love, even an imperfect love that is striving for
greater fullness and truthfulness, there is God.

The sacrament of marriage is not only a blessed sym-
bol of the Covenant which God has offered us in Jesus
Christ; it is also a visible and effective sign of Christ's
own loving presence in and with the husband and wife.
On this point, "The Pastoral Constitution on the Church
in the Modern World" is very explicit:

*Christ our Lord has abundantly blessed this love,
which is rich in its various features, coming as it
does from the spring of divine love and modeled
on Christ's own union with the church. Just as of*

old God encountered his people in a covenant of love and fidelity, so our Savior, the spouse of the church, now encounters christian spouses through the sacrament of marriage. He abides with them in order that by their mutual self-giving spouses will love each other with enduring fidelity, as he loved the church and delivered himself for it.

Gaudium et Spes, 48

The heart of sacramentality is always love that comes from God and leads to God. Everywhere and at all times, marriage has had the great sacramental value of keeping men and women from loneliness and self-centeredness, of involving them in the long human history of a growing love, and growing discernment of what encompasses this noble name. Without this human experience of love in marriage and family, we should probably have no psychological understanding of what a sacrament is.

Marriage is a sacrament not only for the lovers but also for their children, and for their world. The family is the indispensable living and life-giving cell of the Church. Wherever Christians fully live this great covenant of faithful, creative, life-giving, and generous love, they radiate joy and faith, and they help others to become more fully aware of how God comes wonderfully into our lives.

In marriage, human love achieves a unique reciprocity of consciousness through the mutual awareness and mutual appreciation of husband and wife. As they grow increasingly conscious that their own love is a gift of God's love, a new dimension of reciprocity opens to them. They find that the more they love each other, the more they become conscious of and grateful for God's love for them. Christ's healing presence helps couples to accept and to integrate their human failures and limitations, to trust in God's patient work in them.

Christ loves us as we are. He seeks us where we are in order to transform us into masterpieces of his love, in his own image and likeness. The awareness of gradual transformation, becoming ever more a *sacrament,* a visible sign of God's love, leads couples to turn to the Holy Spirit, who alone can transform and renew their hearts and increase their capacity to love.

When husband and wife humbly request and grant each other forgiveness for faults and offenses, and also ask their children to forgive them when they have unjustly blamed or punished them, all—together—come to an awareness of the presence of Christ, healer and reconciler.

Family prayer is a sign that the members of the family truly believe in the Lord's nearness in their daily joys, hopes, and sorrows. There should be, also, the spontaneous sharing of expressions of faith, hope, love, and gratitude, in the various events of their lives.

Christian families who live consciously in God's presence do not confine their love to their own homes; it overflows into the outside world and into many hearts. They are always ready to give friendship to those who are deprived of a home and the warmth of a family. Even those who have chosen or accepted celibacy, are in many ways nourished and sustained by the love-witness of married couples, perhaps especially of their own parents, who were their first witnesses of that life-giving love which comes from God and leads back to God.

Prayer

We thank you, Lord, for all the love, kindness, and patience which your presence has structured into families all over the world and in all religions. We praise you for having made known the source and the goal of all this love to those who believe in you and live a sacrament of love in your honor.

We beg you, Lord, to help those husbands and wives who are experiencing family difficulties. Teach them to love each other, and to love and accept their children and draw them to you. Help them realize that you can, indeed, come into their lives and strengthen them to grow in redeemed and redeeming love.

To all the husbands and wives and parents whose love mirrors your own, grant full consciousness that you alone are the giver of this love, so that they will honor and praise you for it.

Lord, we ask you also to comfort and help those who are unable to build their own marriage and family, and those who are abandoned and live a lonely life. Send them friends, kind and generous people who can become, for them, a sign of your loving presence.

THE PRESENCE OF CHRIST TO THE SICK

It is impressive to see how the sick gained trust and confidence whenever Jesus came. He was totally present to them, with all his loving attention and the healing power of his kindness. Christ is ever present to all, the divine physician who heals us in our human weaknesses, but he wants to manifest his presence in a very special way to those who are suffering or sick.

Through kind and good caregivers, the Lord makes the sick alert to his own compassionate and consoling presence with them. The sacrament of anointing of the sick can have profound significance for sufferers.

Again, presence includes and awakens a reciprocity of consciousness. Not only does Christ want to be present to the sick; he wants them to be present to him, to unite themselves and their suffering with the power of the paschal mystery. Christ comes in the sacrament to meet his suffering friends so that they can become truly aware of him, consciously turn to him, and allow him to insert their suffering into the saving event of his own death and Resurrection.

We all have the mission of helping the sick, especially those who are facing death, making them aware of Christ's redeeming presence with them on their way. When we do this, we are one with Christ who, in the Viaticum, invites the dying to make ready for his final coming.

Prayer

We pray to you, Divine Physician, to illumine and strengthen all of us, and especially those in the healthcare professions, and the friends and relatives of our sick brothers and sisters, so that we may be able to communicate to them the experience of your loving and healing care.

O Christ, let us experience in the crucial moments of our lives that you are near to us and that we can entrust ourselves to you. Strengthen our faith in your paschal mystery, so that those moments which are meaningless without you can receive, through your presence and our response to you, final meaning for us and for the salvation of the world.

The Reign *of* God

The celebration, the sacramental catechesis, and the biblical doctrine on the reign of God illumine each other. In the biblical vision of God's reign, all signs of grace are made visible and understandable.

"Blessed are the poor in spirit" (Matthew 5:3a). The reign of God becomes visible only in servants who, in full awareness and gratitude, live off the primacy of grace. Only those who, in a spirit renewed by the Holy Spirit, acknowledge themselves as God's poor, recognize and accept the reign of God. *"For theirs is the kingdom of heaven"* (Matthew 5:3b).

Scripture speaks of the mystery of the reign of God. Through the economy of salvation, that is, by means of grace and of the full manifestation of God's mercy and goodness, the kingdom is visible. It is a mystery, a *sacrament* revealed to the faithful ones.

The parables on the kingdom express, before all else, the primacy of grace and a corresponding attitude of gratitude, of receptivity, of praise of God, humility, and surrender to God: all this in such faith and trust that the redeemed radiate a new spontaneity, and take new initiatives as they become sharers in God's creative, renewing love. Those who give themselves over to grace bear fruit abundantly. *"Strive for his kingdom, and these things will be given to you as well. Do not be afraid, little flock, for it is your Father's good pleasure to give you the kingdom"* (Luke 12:31-32).

"As we work together with him, we urge you also not to accept the grace of God in vain. For he says, 'At an acceptable time I have listened to you, and on a day of salvation I have helped you.' See, now is the acceptable time; see, now is the day of salvation!"

2 Corinthians 6:1-2

The promise of the reign of God and the celebration of the sacraments urge us to make God's gracious action in us visible through our own generous action in the service of others, so that we too may become sacraments.

Christ rejoices in the mystery of the kingdom: *"I thank you, Father, Lord of heaven and earth, because you have hidden these things from the wise and the intelligent and have revealed them to infants; yes, Father, for such was your gracious will"* (Matthew 11:25-26). But from this assent to the grace of God there arises a more pressing invitation to follow Christ, the servant of God. *"Take my yoke upon you, and learn from me; for I am gentle and humble in heart, and you will find rest for your souls"* (Matthew 11:29).

God's gracious initiative is a call to humility: *"Truly I tell you, unless you change and become like children, you will never enter the kingdom of heaven. Whoever becomes humble like this child is the greatest in the kingdom of heaven"* (Matthew 18:3-4). The acceptance of the reign of God requires generosity and a spirit of sacrifice.

In the paschal mystery, the Word Incarnate reveals to the experience of faith the dynamism of divine trinitarian life. The Father gives himself, with all his wisdom, power, and love, to the Word, his Son. The Word is grace, the revelation of the luminous countenance of the Father. He receives himself from the Father and responds with the gift of himself. The divine life is the life of uncreated grace, an eternal exchange of love in the gift of oneself.

Anointed by the fullness of the Holy Spirit, the human nature of Christ also becomes gift, uniquely graced by union with the Eternal Word. The whole life of Christ expresses gratitude for this unique gift: *"Sacrifices and offerings you have not desired, but a body you have prepared for me....Then I said, 'See, God, I have come to do your will, O God' "* (Hebrews 10:5,7a). And Christ's last breath expresses again the gratitude in the gift of himself: *"Father, into your hands I commend my spirit"* (Luke 23:46b).

Christ reveals the mystery of uncreated grace reflected in his life and death; he insists that his words are not his but the Father's, that he has not come to do his will but the will of him who sent him, and that he has not come to seek his own glory but the glory of the Father. He is confident that the Father, in turn, will glorify him. In the Resurrection, the Father makes visible his full acceptance of Christ's gratitude and trust.

The seven sacraments introduce us, with growing consciousness, to this fundamental meaning of the paschal mystery: of grace made visible in the grateful acceptance of and response to God's gifts. If we consider everything as gift, and want to return to God all the fruits of those gifts, we are already living the divine life and sharing in the mystery of the true God. When we say the sacraments are signs of faith and of grace, we mean that Christ continues his work through the faith and graciousness of those who proclaim the Gospel, who live the Gospel, who share the faith with others and promote the following of Christ.

An authentic sacramental vision does not confine us to seven sacraments, but rather gives us that essential openness that receives, as gifts of God, all events and all opportunities. When we enter fully into the sacramental perspective, all the gifts of God become grace because they bear with them an energy, an appeal, and an invitation from God.

Since all salvation comes from grace, it is impossible to find true communion and solidarity, wholeness and integrity, except in the explicit recognition of God's gifts to us.

It is from the primacy of grace and the nature of God's reign that the Gospel gives meaning to morality. The primacy of grace demands that the sacramental celebration and the whole *kerygma* be, above all, an effective evangelization. Grace is the revelation of the face of God. Grace is the saving and energizing event.

Every teaching, and every sacramental celebration should turn our attention to the Covenant between Christ and his Church, between God and humankind: an alliance which is a gratuitous gift and, in its gratuitousness, calls for a total commitment to God, and to God's design to gather all people in a Covenant of gracious, gentle, and generous love.

Part Two

Signs
of
Faith

The Words
of The Word

Any treatment of the sacraments as real and effica-cious signs of faith has to avoid two dangers: It can either underestimate the privileged role of the sacra-ments in the economy of grace, or overrate it in such a way as to make God's work and our faith seem to be a monopoly of the sacraments.

An authentic listening to God in the Scriptures and in the liturgy opens our eyes, heart, and mind, and thus allows us to perceive this God who speaks through all things. The whole of creation and of redemption, all the forms of God's active presence in history, have the charac-ter of Word. They are the revelation and communication of God to all who can understand and respond in faith.

Christ himself is the great sacrament of redemption. The seven sacraments tend to open us to the mystery of Christ in an ever-growing faith, so that our lives become more and more a listening and response to God.

In the sacraments, we sense the nearness of God. As the sacraments help us to find and to understand our true selves, we gradually grasp the message communi-cated to us by the whole created universe, especially by the love and needs of our sisters and brothers.

The sacraments are a marvelous message of joy, a communion; thus, they effectively challenge us to trea-sure and give thanks for the gifts they bestow. God gifts us with the joyous incentive to a new life.

The whole liturgy has the character of listening to God's Word and responding to it as wholeheartedly as possible in our individual and communal lives. The words of the sacraments want to make us mature hearers of God's Word as it reaches us in the sacramental celebration, in Scripture, in all creation and history, and in all the events of life. Only when we learn to listen with attentive and ready hearts can we truly celebrate, with the Church, the liturgical response to God's gifts and words.

All the sacraments, as signs and gifts which have their meaning and force only through their intimate relation to Christ's sacrifice and that of the Church, are signs of the Covenant. Christ's sacrifice is, par excellence, the sign and seal of the Covenant. In every sacrament, this universal meaning is actualized and communicated to this specific community, this particular individual. To receive a sacrament is to respond with a solemn "Yes" to the Covenant *as it applies to our particular life.* We accept, in gratitude, the grace and the law of the Covenant as direction for all of life. Faith, therefore, includes orthopraxis as much as orthodoxy.

In that which is their essence, the sacraments signify the new and eternal Covenant, given us through no merit of our own, and the response of all who, in faith, recognize the grace of the Covenant. This response is united with that of Jesus Christ. The liturgy effectively introduces us to the dialogue between God and humankind by a progressive education in living faith. The sign becomes all the more effective the more we become ready to accept the grace, and to respond with all our hearts.

Every power and capacity of Christian life originates

from the dialogue of the Covenant, from a faith which keeps us in vital contact with God, and with the people of the Covenant within the community of faith.

COMMUNAL AND PERSONAL DIALOGUE

The biblical idea of Covenant and the continuous living experience given to it by the liturgy instruct the faithful on the nature of Christian life. Christian life is a dialogue which is fully personal and at the same time fully communitarian.

Every believer receives the grace of faith in the community of faith. The sacraments do not consign us to some secluded spot for souls to be alone with God, separated from the community. Instead, they turn the whole person to God in a community of faith, hope, and love. The Covenant to which we respond individually is the Covenant of God with the community of the redeemed, of Christ with his Church.

The sign of the Covenant calls us together in the ecclesial community—a sacrament of unity for the whole of humankind—and our response is valid and just only in the community and in view of the community. From a true liturgical concelebration arises the acute consciousness that even the silent prayer—in the depths of our hearts, in the privacy of our homes, in the whole of our lives—is *in profound communion with all people*, living and dead.

We pray truthfully only when we say "Our Father" in familial love and reverence for all people. We can say "I believe in one God" only if we are working for peace and unity in the world. We can claim to "believe in one holy, catholic, apostolic church" only insofar as we are trying, in solidarity and cooperation, to make the Church a visible sign of the oneness of humanity. The liturgy, by its very essence, teaches us that there is no opposition between the fundamental social-communitarian aspect of salvation and the true personalism of faith.

Liturgical dialogue, being a dialogue of faith and adoring love, is personal. The personalism of each member, however, is authentically deepened as the love and unity increase in all members of the community to which God speaks. Both together, then—the member and the community—give a life-response. A personal life and a truly communitarian life thus become one in our adoring response to God's love. One cannot be obtained without the other.

The liturgy is one of the privileged schools of this truth. If we neglect it, we have little hope of learning the fundamental components of Christian life, since in Christ's intention the Eucharist and the other sacraments are the favored sources of growth in faith and in undivided love, justice, and peace. The intrinsic unity of the love of God and of neighbor requires, therefore, a truly communal celebration of the liturgy which is demanded by the very nature of the sacraments. They call for truth of life, and this reveals what the manner of celebration should be.

Prayer

We believe that only through the undeserved gift of the Spirit can we come to truthful adoration of your name, O Lord. When the Spirit dwells in us and we docilely accept that divine presence, we can, in joy and in truth, call you "our Father."

But we know, through your revelation, that your abundant gifts and promises do not allow us to be lazy. You ask—and make possible—our creative cooperation.

Make us grateful, Lord. Make us vigilant, so that each of us, within our families and our communities, may join hands and energies to create the best possible conditions for the synthesis of faith and life, of prayer and service to our sisters and brothers.

MYSTERY OF FAITH AND SALVATION

The sacraments are to be considered as efficacious signs of faith, through Christ and the Holy Spirit, and thus in and with the faith of the Church. *Faith is itself a sacramental reality.* Its saving efficacy comes from Christ, the great sacrament. In the words and the sacramental rites, Christ himself is the faithful witness who reassures us that he came for us, died and is risen for us. By the sacraments in the community of faith, and by the light of grace, God gives to our eyes and our mind proof that the mysteries of salvation save us, gather us, if we loyally open ourselves to them in faith.

The sacraments are saving events only for those who believe and yearn for an increase of faith. The one who does not believe and does not want to believe receives the sacraments insincerely. Unless one wants to live a life of faith and according to faith, one receives the sacraments fruitlessly, scorning the fecundity of faith which is that experience of God's gracious love that engenders a creative, gracious, and generous life-response.

The sacramental celebration signifies that the Church—actual, here and now, in the celebrating assembly—listens and responds to the action of God with its humble confession and joyous profession of faith. Those who receive the sacraments in a spirit of faith and in a desire for increase of faith are justified by that faith which God awakens and brings to fuller life through the sacred signs and symbols. Awakened faith is the dynamic answer of the Church, in each of its members, in the celebration of the sacraments. The result will be a life of thanksgiving to God.

The authentic disposition for genuine sacramental dialogue with Christ is an attitude expressed in the prophet's words, *"Here am I; send me"* (Isaiah 6:8b); an attitude of eagerness to hear the words of The Word, and to act on them in response to the gifts of God, and to all the testimony and revelation of God's faithful love. God's signs are deeds, events; they are active, alive; and so should be our response.

The Church honors God by a profession of faith informed by love. Living by the life-giving words of the Incarnate Word, the community and every one of its members is destined to a eucharistic faith that is full of love and gratitude. Normally, therefore, the sacraments will be all the more fruitful the more the ecclesial community joyfully and gratefully communicates its faith to every member.

The universal Church is actualized in the local church, which arouses and sustains the faith of its individual members. The Church, both universal and local, contributes to the disposition of every person according to its degree of faith.

A true dialogue of faith is possible only when there is full acceptance of the gifts of God—on the part of the community and of every single member in it. That the sacraments of faith be considered in this vision is of paramount importance for ecumenical dialogue. We will then realize that whatever is good comes from the one Father, through his Son, as gift of the one Spirit, and will therefore be watchful for all signs of faith and love which we find in other churches, and even in non-Christian religions.

With equal insistence, the Gospel teaches the regenerating power of both faith and sacraments. Of baptism and Eucharist, Jesus said: *"Very truly, I tell you, no one can enter the kingdom of God without being born of water and Spirit"* (John 3:5); and, *"Those who eat my flesh and drink my blood abide in me, and I in them"* (John 6:56). The same saving power is recognized for faith: *"But to all who received him, who believed in his name, he gave power to become children of God"* (John 1:12) in order *"that whoever believes in him may have eternal life"* (John 3:15). These two lines of thought, namely, of faith that saves and of the sacraments that bring salvation, ought never to be separated.

As in the intimacy of friendship, the love which is given and that which is received form a unified reality. Analogously, in the sacraments of faith, the action of God that reveals and offers gifts tends to become one with the acceptance of those gifts by all who respond with a living, active faith.

It follows that our whole moral and religious life depends on and subsists in the words of The Word. It arises from the Covenant of love and develops in dialogue with a faith informed by—or at least tending to express itself in—redeemed love. It follows, also, that the gifts common to the whole people of the Covenant, as well as those given to individual persons, are always accepted and understood in view of the community. They are, in a strict sense, gifts and messages which oblige the members of the new Covenant to a greater dedication in co-responsibility for the good of all.

Thus, only when the sacramental spirituality leads us to a sacramental vision of all the works of God, the signs of the times and the concrete opportunity of the *kairos,* and when all of creation is for us—in the light of the Word Incarnate—truly a word and an appeal, does the sacramental morality dynamically open to us new and radiant horizons.

Prayer

Lord Jesus Christ, we believe that you are risen and are our Savior, the Lord of the whole world. We believe that you seek us, that you are always present to us if only we make ourselves present to you. Send forth your Spirit, that our hearts may be purified and our eyes opened to your coming.

Give us friends in the community of believers. Help us to become a holy, prayerful people, so that we can help each other to discover the dimensions and the bliss of your presence. Make us vigilant, O Lord, for your coming.

Part Three

Signs
of
Hope

Hope *and* Virtues

The sacraments, as we have considered them, are efficacious signs of the reign of God. The reign of God is, however, essentially an *eschatological reality*, a reality of the future world and a reality already present. So the sacraments too have an eschatological significance.

What specifically belongs to Christian eschatology is posed clearly in the light of the sacraments. Christian life is directed to the perfect state of glory, not chiefly by a relation of desire or of merit, but more by grateful awareness of what God has already prepared and by vigilance toward the present opportunities; by that hope which arises from the experience of faith in the ongoing presence of God and makes us ready for Christ's coming.

The sacraments, as they are mysteries of faith, are also mysteries and efficacious signs of hope—*"For in hope we were saved"* (Romans 8:24a). Through the sacraments, the present moment of grace and our current decisions move into the perspective of the history of salvation. For the faithful who make use of the immediate opportunities, the sacraments are signs of this *"day of salvation"* (see 2 Corinthians 6:2) which has been manifested ever since the first coming of Christ, and a pledge of hope that the fruitfulness of grace will be fully manifested in the *parousia*. The celebration of the sacraments of hope opens broad horizons to a genuine vision of history.

An understanding of the sacraments cannot be authentic if they are limited to mere remembrance of past events, or to the consolation that arises from an expectation of future bliss. The sacramental memorial is not merely a narration of past events, but is a vital insertion into Christ. The intention of the sacraments is to make us actors of hope in the history of redemption and liberation of the whole world.

In the celebration of the pledges of hope, the redemption of the present moment becomes urgent and possible. In recognizing the present gift, we see better possibilities of love of neighbor for insertion into the community of redeeming love.

In this way, with a serenity that flows from trust and gratitude, and with that efficient dynamism that discovers the precious pearl of the reign of God in the vast field of history, we are on our way to *"the city of the living God, the heavenly Jerusalem"* (Hebrews 12:22b). In celebration of gratitude in hope, we profit by the warning: *"See that you do not refuse the one who is speaking"* (Hebrews 12:25a).

There follows the unequalled importance of gratitude in Christian life. The purposeful dynamism of Christian life arises from the salvific presence of the Lord of history and from the grace already received and responded to by gratitude.

True and effective hope is bound to both the present opportunities and the promised reality with a eucharistic spirit that "gives thanks, always and everywhere" for the harvest of grace and the abundant salvation already made manifest. But the gifts already received direct all our energies and all the present opportunities to the final goal.

"Not that I have already obtained this or have already reached the goal; but I press on to make it my own, because Christ Jesus has made me his own....I press on toward the goal for the prize of the heavenly call of God in Christ Jesus."

Philippians 3:12,14

When the vivifying Spirit speaks to us through the sacraments, we recognize—in the humbleness of our time—the time of grace, in the heart of which beat the strengths and virtues of the death, Resurrection, and promise of the *Parousia*. Thus appears the importance of vigilance, which occupies a central place among the eschatological virtues. Vigilance for the present opportunities, and unfailing courage to resist the temptations of evasion, are marks of Christ's pressing love working in us. We are vigilant if we recognize the coming of the Lord in the talents that are entrusted to us, and in the needs of our neighbor and of the community that cry out to us for help.

The fruitfulness of the liturgy grows when we learn to translate the expression of our hope into living witness of the One who was, who is, and who is to come. This is only possible if, in its expressions, liturgy never loses contact with real life.

"Why do you stand looking up toward heaven?"(Acts of the Apostles 1:11b). Eschatological expectation ought to stimulate in us intense zeal for a more humane world, a zeal which has to be rooted and nourished in a spirit of faith and prayer. The ultimate tension of Christian life, enlivened by sacramental spirituality, will not be misguided by any apocalyptic calculation of the day or hour

of the *Parousia*. Its dynamic teaches us, rather, to look to the fertility of the here-and-now in the light of our last moments and final expectations.

True eschatological perspective of one's life, fruit of a sacramental spirituality, knows how to reconcile true respect for human traditions with a courageous openness to new forms of customs and cultures. The fidelity and continuity which are the living expressions of all the eschatological virtues leave no room for either an immobile clinging to traditions or a restless discontinuity and sensationalism.

Joy is a characteristic virtue of the sacramental person. Here we take the word "virtue" in its original meaning of strength and dynamism. We have seen how the sacraments, signs of grace, reflect the face of God. Therefore, they transform us into visible signs of grace by means of goodness. Joy connotes serenity, graciousness, and gentleness. That kind of sadness, sorrow, and seriousness that stifles our real humanity has nothing to do with Christian hope, since it veils the gracious presence of God in us.

The sacraments are visible signs of hope for the whole world only through the joy with which the believer and the whole community of faith receive the happy tidings which they symbolize. Where there is no joy, there is no testimony to the strength of faith.

In the celebration of the sacraments of faith, Christian hope is nurtured and deepened in joy, *"for the joy of the LORD is your strength"* (Nehemiah 8:10b). Although the eschatological times to which the sacraments commit us are marked by struggle and final separation,

Christian hope becomes, by those same sacraments, a source of joy and serenity.

Eschatological hope embraces and transforms the critical sense and, also, all the hopes of the secular city. The eschatological dimension develops, in Christians, the prophetic sense of constructive criticism and of discernment. The virtue of criticism, of veritable discernment, springs from a live celebration of the great events of salvation history, where all people are drawn into one hope, and search together for an ever more effective witness to this hope. Believers, in the sacraments of hope, exercise criticism only with a compassionate love for all.

Hope's Purpose
and Power

The grace of the Covenant urges believers to carry on to the end—together—on the road which Christ traveled to the end, in his most radical expression of solidarity with all people.

All the sacraments proclaim that the source of our hope is in the "one baptism" which Christ took upon himself on the altar of the cross. Ritually and sacramentally, it was prefigured by his baptism in the Jordan during a general baptism of the people (see Luke 3:21). In his baptism, he is side by side with all the sinners who, by the Spirit, learn that they are poor: He bears the burden of all so that all may learn the same law (see Galatians 6:2). When we celebrate, in the sacraments, the "one baptism" which is the source of all hope, we learn to become of one heart in love. As Saint Augustine reminded his faithful: "You, my beloved, you are sacraments of salvation, if all your life makes visible what Christ in the sacraments has made visible to us."

The Church is the ark of salvation and the pledge of hope in its charity and unity. The liturgical celebrations are celebrations of the Church which is the sacrament of unity. The whole sacramental *kerygma* makes us conscious of this urgency: *"There is one body and one Spirit, just as you were called to the one hope of your calling, one Lord, one faith, one baptism"* (Ephesians 4:4-5).

The salvation and dignity of the individual person

reside in the hope of salvation of the people of God, and are thus authentic and safe. The sacramental signs, as prognostic signs that envision the blessed communion of saints, are at the same time signs of communitarian hope that lead the faithful to a common commitment.

COSMIC HOPE

Eschatological hope, as signified and proclaimed in the sacraments, cannot be restricted to the soul and the resurrection of the body, nor even to the whole community. It has also a cosmic aspect, in that it includes the world which is entrusted to us and is involved in our failures and achievements. Redemption and hope extend to the whole created universe, particularly to the environmental world.

This aspect of hope and commitment is signified by the use of precious elements of the earth—the "work of human hands," water, bread, wine, oil—in the liturgy. All these signs speak to us of the consecration of world and life. These symbols turn our attention to that broader concept of the sacramentality of all creation and all history: They indicate and make mandatory a new perspective and a firm commitment to justice and holiness in all our lives.

In the liturgy, we look forward, with an ever greater desire and increasing hope, to *"a new heaven and a new earth"* (Revelation 21:1a), for *"the creation waits with eager longing for the revealing of the children of God"* (Romans 8:19). To believers, this means grace, and a mandate to commit ourselves, individually and in solidarity, to the humanization and redemption of the whole economic, social, and cultural life: to work for liberation and reconciliation on all levels. Awareness that the full liberty of the sons and daughters of God, and the full redemption of the world, will be granted only in the *Parousia*, will prevent wrong messianic hopes, as well as acts of violence. Christians who are shaped by the sacraments of hope will work untiringly, with patience and nonviolence.

Through all the sacramental signs, especially the rites of blessing of those things which the liturgy uses for the sacraments, we are reminded that sin tends to break the salvific solidarity of humanity with the cosmos and with all the other creatures of God. The sacraments make us conscious of the new and urgent task of human solidarity on an environmental and cosmic scale, which arises from the very fact that we are redeemed. A true liturgical spirituality stirs our most authentic energies for the redemption of the world. Those who do not give attention to the proper environmental aspect of the sacramental graces cannot bear fruit fully, even in other fields.

Prayer

Lord, you are the great artist. Day by day you carry on your great work of forming us into your masterpieces, images of your own goodness and kindness. It is for this that you send us rain as well as sunshine, suffering as well as pure joy.

So you call each of us by a unique name; your love for me is always love for my neighbor too. Grant that I—that we—may be signs of your coming, of your being with us and accomplishing your work of transforming us into signs of your goodness, of your presence.

BAPTISM AND HOPE

The seven sacraments are, altogether, exalted eschatological signs of the pilgrim Church, but each one of them has its particular signification, its specific grace, and thus communicates a particular task. The import of the signs and words of the sacraments, together with the total experience of the people of God in pilgrimage, reveal the inexhaustible riches and the royal mandate which derives from the grace of God. This will be all the more evident as the sacramental life becomes more integrated with the life experience of those who bear witness to Christian hope.

Baptism is a celebration of faith and of hope in the community of salvation in Christ. We experience in baptism our personal insertion into the new and eternal Covenant, as members of the chosen people. We are united in one hope, in view of common profession and testimony of faith and hope, and in view of a common eschatological struggle. Baptism derives all its meaning from the "one baptism" Christ endured for all. It *"raised us up with him and seated us with him in the heavenly places in Christ Jesus"* (Ephesians 2:6), insofar as it enables us on earth to suffer with Christ, so sharing his solidarity and his mission to bring Good News to the poor.

Through the living, signified reality of the grace and task of baptism, we have a share in that reign which Christ has revealed as the servant of all, if we, in turn, learn how to serve and to carry the burdens of others.

Baptism makes us conscious of the common battle that must be waged against the forces of darkness, sin, and threatening evil power. This is the reason for the exorcisms and baptismal pledges. The saints who live according to the grace of baptism, always conscious of its meaning, give everywhere a living testimony of the hope of glory, which in no way allows an alienation from proper aspirations in the social realm.

Those who, in Christ, have become *"a new creation"* (2 Corinthians 5:17a) announce the new heaven and new earth in which the power of all idols will be broken. Sealed with the blood of the new and everlasting Covenant, they are no longer slaves of a self-centered world that passes away.

The "already" of faith and baptism points forward to the end, but it does so by drawing grateful attention to the decisive events of the past—the Incarnation, passion, death and Resurrection, and the outpouring of the Spirit. However, the perspective points more dynamically toward the future, as the believer receives, with open mind and heart, the gift of the Spirit, and is incorporated into the Body of Christ (see 1 Corinthians 12:13). The sometimes painful experience of the "not yet" in healthy tension with the "already" has a decisive influence on the lives of believers, to the extent that it intensifies their consciousness of being coworkers with Christ, carrying out the saving plan in history. This is what characterizes our ethical decisions if we live according to the dynamics of baptism.

Prayer

Lord, you have given us parents to reveal to us your kindness and your tender love. Each day you send us friends who, by their gentleness,

draw our attention to you. You send us people
who are so generous that only you can be the
source and the fulfillment of their good will. You
allow us to meet people who receive us and
encourage us, and so help us to experience your
love, which gives us our greatest hope. You send
us people who listen to us and understand us.
Then we know again that you always listen to
us and understand us. You are always with us,
Lord. You call us and wait for us. Make us
grateful; make us alert.

CONFIRMATION AND HOPE

The very name, *Christ* ("Anointed") is linked to the
outpouring of the Spirit which manifests the coming of
the messianic age. John the Baptist was aware of this:
"He on whom you see the Spirit descend and remain is
the one who baptizes with the Holy Spirit" (John 1:33b).
The outpouring of the Spirit at the Pentecost event was,
for Peter, proof that the hoped-for messianic age had
come:

"In the last days it will be, God declares, that I
will pour out my Spirit upon all flesh, and your
sons and your daughters shall prophesy....Even
upon my slaves, both men and women, in those
days I will pour out my Spirit; and they shall
prophesy."

Acts of the Apostles 2:17a,18 (see also Joel 2:28)

We should, in this context, not forget that the charism
of the prophets is integration between life and faith: a

holistic vision of love of God and of neighbor, maturity, and discernment.

Those baptized by the Spirit, and who let themselves be led by the Spirit, can hope in the midst of suffering and trial, *"and hope does not disappoint us, because God's love has been poured into our hearts through the Holy Spirit that has been given to us"* (Romans 5:5). Since the Spirit is their life, they experience the inner freedom to use the present opportunities and to look forward to the final fulfillment of their life. This freedom makes believers attentive to the groaning of creation to have its share. The spiritual person lives in full solidarity with the hopes and struggles of all people, of the whole created universe—a witness to the liberating power and creativity of a life under the guidance of the Holy Spirit.

Prayer

Teach us how to pray, O Lord. Teach us how to transform all our lives into adoration of the Father "in spirit and in truth." Send us your Spirit, to help us become fully sincere in our prayer and in the shaping of our daily lives and social commitments. Cleanse us from our sins, from selfishness and superficiality. Help us to progress in the knowledge that is eternal life, in knowing that you alone are truly God, and Jesus Christ whom you have sent.

EUCHARIST AND HOPE

"And they shall all be taught by God" (John 6:45). In Christ's discourse on the Eucharist and on faith, it is clear that faith in the Eucharist and its hope-inspiring

dynamics are thoroughly linked to the outpouring of the Spirit. *"Then what if you were to see the Son of Man ascending to where he was before? It is the spirit that gives life; the flesh is useless. The words that I have spoken to you are spirit and life"* (John 6:62-63).

The Eucharist has to be seen in the light of the Covenant theology, which already in the great messianic prophesies points to the Spirit (see Jeremiah 31:31; Exodus 37:1-14), and which is the heart of the Pauline gospel. The celebration of the new and everlasting Covenant in the Eucharist is a prophetic event through the Spirit, filled with hope. It is through the Spirit that Christ, the Covenant, has lived, even unto death, the truth of love and solidarity. It is through the same Spirit that bread and wine become for us the body and blood of Christ, so that we become one body and one spirit, and can enter fully into the prophetic event and Covenant of Christ's sacrificial death and Resurrection.

Since the Eucharist is the work of the Holy Spirit, only spiritual persons, guided by the Spirit and thus filled with hope for the banquet of eternal life, are prepared for Christ's promise: *"and I will raise them up on the last day"* (John 6:54b)—which, again, is the work of the Spirit.

The form of festive banquet proper to the Eucharist obviously reminds us of the value of the prognostic sign of the heavenly banquet. It comes through clearly in various biblical texts. For the institution of the Eucharist, Christ chose *"a large room upstairs, furnished and ready"* (Mark 14:15a). The parables on the wedding banquet (Matthew 8:11; 25:10-13; Luke 14:15), in which many from the East and from the West will participate, begin to be realized—in the eucharistic banquet—as prefiguring and preparing for the eternal banquet of the Lamb with his bride (see Revelation 19:6-9).

However, in these parables that illustrate the festive character of the Eucharist, there is never lacking the aspect of mystery. Only those who are ready and alert, who recognize the Lord in the poor, who are wearing the nuptial gown and have in hand the lighted lamps, will be admitted to the banquet of eternal life. The eschatological separation, already going on, is hope-inspiring only for those who fear the Lord with that holy fear which bears fruit in love and justice for the life of the world.

Prayer

Lord, you have promised us wonderful things: that we shall always be with you. All that you have done and entrusted to us is a part of your promise, a sign of your faithfulness. You have promised the beatitude of a life where you are, with all our sisters and brothers, all your children.

Now, in this in-between time, you are our Way. You are on the road with us, the road that leads to you and the final joy of your presence. Lord, you are always near to us; you call us and wait for us. Make us grateful; make us ready.

RECONCILIATION AND HOPE

The eschatological significance of this sacrament is to be seen in its intimate connection with baptism and Eucharist. Each of us and all of us are in constant need of further purification and conversion. The ministry of the Church's members is clear: *"We are ambassadors for Christ, since God is making his appeal through us; we entreat you on behalf of Christ, be reconciled to God"* (2 Corinthians 5:20).

The Church is meant to be in constant process of purification and reconciliation. The more it is conscious of this need, and humbly confesses its shortcomings, the better it will carry out a task similar to that of John the Baptist: *"to turn the hearts of parents to their children, and the disobedient to the wisdom of the righteous, to make ready a people prepared for the Lord"* (Luke 1:17b). The polarizations and tensions within the Church and society, and even within each family and community, should be brought into the full light and healing power of Christ's patience. Then they can inspire genuine hope and a common striving toward fulfillment of the great eschatological command: *"Be merciful, just as your Father is merciful"* (Luke 6:36). In other words: *"Be perfect, therefore, as your heavenly Father is perfect"* (Matthew 5:48).

The sacrament of reconciliation gives new strength to those who are wounded and weakened in the eschatological battle. It aspires to transform all into instruments of peace and nonviolence, and it cures the sick members of the Church. By its healing word, the sacrament reconciles those who were harmful and contagious members, and readmits them to the eucharistic banquet, thus strengthening all in the hope for the heavenly banquet.

Prayer

O Lord, you lead us to those who are in sorrow and in need of comfort. You come in the guise of the poor and allow us to make them rich with your goodness. You bring to us those who are disillusioned and discouraged, so that we may be a sign of your consolation and encouragement.

You send us, O Lord, at the same time, so many gifts of your goodness, and those who are in need of love, so that we may transform your love into love for our sisters and brothers; so that, all together, we can experience that you are always with us, that you call us and wait for us. Lord, make us vigilant and generous. All our life waits for your final coming.

GRACE AND HOPE

With Christ's own love, the sacraments urge us to grow in love of God and neighbor, and enable us better to discern true love from its counterfeits. The New Testament command to "be perfect" is the normative invitation to all disciples, *"according to the measure of Christ's gift"* (Ephesians 4:7b) granted to each person in these final ages.

Christian holiness is a firm commitment to strive with all one's powers toward the goal defined by the fullness of the times. To the rich young man (see Matthew 19:16-21), it is not said that to enter into eternal life he may choose between keeping the old commandments or becoming perfect. Rather, it is said that to make the necessary transition from the old economy to the fullness of the times, he must free himself completely and follow the Lord.

In the Letter to the Philippians, the apostle refutes any static concept of Christian perfection. No one stands perfect. Those who are Christians untiringly *"press on....forgetting what lies behind and straining forward to what lies ahead"* (Philippians 3:12b,13b).

The sacraments instruct us in the law of continuous growth. They tell us that we must strive constantly *"to make it [our] own, because Christ Jesus has made [us] his own"* (Philippians 3:12c). Thus we live in faith according to that justice by which God graciously justifies us. With Paul, we long to know Christ, to experience the power of his Resurrection, and to share his sufferings in growing conformity with his death, *"if somehow I may attain the resurrection from the dead"* (Philippians 3:11). Thus, the true and effective goal stems from the law of grace which reveals the meaning of the history of salvation.

Prayer

*Lord, make us vigilant and generous. All our life
waits for your final coming. With complete trust
we look forward to the hour of your call. You
yourself will come, will call us each by name.
Then we shall know that your judgment is
salvation and compassion if we but faithfully
respond to your coming whenever and wherever
you call us through our sisters and brothers,
through the poor.*

*Come, Lord Jesus, call whenever you want,
under whatever conditions you decide. Abide
with us. Make us vigilant and ready for your
coming. Maranatha.*

Part Four

Signs

of

Adoration

Adoration *in* Spirit *and* Truth

All sacraments are primarily worship. The communal celebration of the sacrament of reconciliation, especially when it culminates in a final act of thanksgiving and praise for divine mercy, returns to this sacrament the cultic dimension which it had lost before Vatican II.

When Jesus, speaking with the Samaritan woman, comes to the critical subject of how her life would and should be transformed, she escapes into a formalistic question typical of an age of sacralization: *"Our ancestors worshiped on this mountain, but you say that the place where people must worship is in Jerusalem"* (John 4:20). The Lord's response explains how the whole of life, in all its dimensions, ought to become true worship of the living God.

> *"Woman, believe me, the hour is coming when you will worship the Father neither on this mountain nor in Jerusalem....But the hour is coming, and is now here, when the true worshipers will worship the Father in spirit and truth, for the Father seeks such as these to worship him. God is spirit, and those who worship him must worship in spirit and truth."*
>
> John 4:21,23-24

These words certainly are not intended to confirm a spiritualism that scorns the visible world and visible signs; however, they do exclude any monopoly of worship on behalf of sacred places or of specific liturgical celebrations. They decisively transcend a ritualism and formalism which trust only in an exact repetition of rites and formulas.

Central to true worship is conversion to God, the one Father of all, and to Christ, in whom God has willed to show the full splendor of divine love and justice, and by whom the Father has been truly adored and glorified in a love that returns all of humankind to God.

While the sacraments of the Church express, in a privileged and unique way, that it is the God we honor who enables and teaches us to do so, they are not the only signs used to reveal divine glory and invite us to adoration. Adoration of God in spirit and truth is based on the synthesis between individual conversion and social renewal, reform of Church and social justice; the integration of prayer and life. It is fully realized only in Christ, whom the Holy Spirit has anointed for the final revelation of the plentitude of goodness, justice, and mercy of the Father, and for the response of true worship.

The Temple of Jerusalem was the privileged place in which the fidelity and mercy of God was revealed. God invited the people to gather, as people of the Covenant, to honor God with unity in worship. However, the people often gave a monopolistic significance to the Temple. On the other hand, the whole history of the prophets was a continuous call to the adoration of God throughout one's life.

"Do not trust in these deceptive words: 'This is the temple of the LORD, the temple of the LORD, the temple of the LORD.' For if you truly amend your ways and your doings, if you truly act justly one with another, if you do not oppress the alien, the orphan, and the widow, or shed innocent blood in this place, and if you do not go after other gods to your own hurt, then I will dwell with you in this place, in the land that I gave of old to your ancestors forever and ever."

Jeremiah 7:4-7

The sacraments of the "new law" forbid all sterile ritualism which, in a scrupulous uniformity of formulas and rubrics, exhausts the energies of the people. On the contrary, the sacraments are privileged signs through which God gives, to persons and communities, the ability to render honor and thanks; and not only in the celebration itself, but in lives of fidelity to the great realities communicated in the sacraments—lives that can be truly offered as worship of the Father, in union with Christ, and as harvest of the Spirit.

We should so celebrate *baptism* that all believers experience their unity in the "one baptism" in which Christ has honored the Father by manifesting his total solidarity with all people, drawing all to unity. Baptism will thus generate children of God who become one in Christ, that the world may believe in and honor one God, becoming more humane and just.

The sacrament of *reconciliation* should thus exemplify the encounter with Christ, our peace and reconciliation, that more and more we become channels of peace and ambassadors of reconciliation, in praise of the God who has reconciled the world in Jesus Christ.

Preparation for the diaconate and *priesthood*, and the election or nomination of bishops and popes, should be geared to their main mission: to be persons who, in an outstanding way, have reached the integration of faith and life, of prayer and familial love, and thus can help all the faithful to better realize what it means to adore God in spirit and truth.

Participation in the *Eucharist*, and in all the liturgical life of the Church, should give us such a vital and deep experience of worship, praise, and thanksgiving in community that at all times we make our choices for all the right reasons: to offer our thoughts, desires, and actions to God as praise and thanksgiving with Christ, and unite our burdens with his sacrifice.

Anointing of the sick should be understood and celebrated in such a way that Christians become able to offer their suffering and pain, and especially their death—with Christ—to the praise of the Father and for the salvation of the world.

The sacrament of *confirmation* should be oriented to the formation of mature Christians who, in solidarity, discernment, generosity, creative liberty, and fidelity, can manifest to the world what a true adorer of God is meant to be.

In the sacrament of *matrimony*, spouses accept one another as gifts of God, and offer each other and their children that love, patience, forbearance, and respect that truly render thanks to the Giver of all good gifts.

Be filled with the Spirit, as you sing psalms and hymns and spiritual songs among yourselves, singing and making melody to the Lord in your hearts, giving thanks to God the Father at all times and for everything in the name of our Lord Jesus Christ. Be subject to one another out of reverence for Christ.

Ephesians 5:18b-21

Prayer

Lord, you are always with us; you come constantly into our lives; you wait for our coming to you. From you, each day anew, we receive our names, our lives, our capacity to love. All and everything is your gift, a message of your love, a sign of your coming.

Lord, you are always with us; you call us and wait always for us. In all our joys, in the light of the sun, in the immensity of the firmament, in a child's smile, a mother's kindness, a father's strength, it is always you who come to meet us and to call us. Make us grateful and vigilant.

The Virtue *of* Religion

The sacraments point to God's initiative. A sacramental spirituality emphasizes the cultic aspect of the sacraments of faith, hope, and love. The sacraments properly serve the unique dynamism of lives inspired by that same faith, hope, and love, for the greater glory of God. Our sanctification renders us capable of lives fully united to Christ—Redeemer, High Priest, Prophet, and Universal Sacrament of Love.

The "law of sanctity" is the power of grace which emanates from the dynamic revelation of God's holiness and is inscribed in us as law: *"You shall be holy, for I the LORD your God am holy"* (Leviticus 19:2b). The priestly law of holiness in the Hebrew Scriptures embraces, at the same time, explicit worship and all familial relations—not only with the "chosen people," but also and above all with the migrants and aliens—so that they may recognize the one God in their lives. Those who have been "chosen" experience the revelation of God's holiness, and also receive a consecration to a mission of glorification of God before all nations. The law of holiness calls for a life of relationships.

> *You shall not hate in your heart anyone of your kin; you shall reprove your neighbor, or you will incur guilt yourself. You shall not take vengeance or bear a grudge against any of your people, but*

you shall love your neighbor as yourself: I am the LORD.

Leviticus 19:17-18

The sacraments are more than a school of worship; they are, above all, acts of Christ that, by means of the Holy Spirit, enable us to be united to his worship in spirit and truth.

For the grace of God has appeared, bringing salvation to all, training us to renounce impiety and worldly passions, and in the present age to live lives that are self-controlled, upright, and godly, while we wait for the blessed hope and the manifestation of the glory of our great God and Savior, Jesus Christ.

Titus 2:11-13

What the Letter to Titus attributes to the grace made visible in the Word Incarnate, can also be applied to the sacraments in their intimate relation to Christ. Instructed and formed by the grace of the sacraments, we see, in all God's signs and gifts, an appeal and an invitation to adore the Lord in spirit and truth.

THE SACRAMENTS AS WORSHIP

The sacraments insert us into the community of worship—the Church—which, in Christ and through his Spirit, is a sacrament of salvation for the whole of humankind because it is called to be a sacrament of adoration in spirit and truth.

By means of the Church—which is the sacrament of encounter with Christ—the Christian enters into intimate friendship with him, and participates in the consecrating power of his passion and Resurrection, by which the whole of human history becomes the economy of salvation, giving glory to God the Father in the unity of the Holy Spirit. Inserted in Christ, the believer becomes a participant in Christ's own gift of self, offered to the Father in the Holy Spirit. Thus the sacramental life unites us initially to the *heavenly liturgy*.

By means of the sacraments received in a spirit of worship, the believer becomes holy (that is, consecrated to truthful adoration of God) in his/her most intimate existence, in all relationships with neighbor(s) and the world, and in all the essential aspects of his/her life.

The sacraments "ordain" us to social worship because we have become *"a priestly kingdom and a holy nation"* (Exodus 19:6b; see also 1 Peter 2:9). Through the grace and the mandate of the sacraments, we are informed, and we receive power to carry out the mission of ordaining the whole of our lives in ways that give praise to the grace and glory of God. Through charity and social justice, especially toward our enemies, we render a true cult to God and can say in truth, "Our Father."

The sacraments are means of personal and social salvation inasmuch as they instruct us and give us competence to live our individual and social lives in that spirit of responsibility and commitment which is a truly acceptable offering to the glory of God. In the intention of Christ, the liturgy is a preeminent school that effectively introduces us to a life which can bridge the gap between religion and life, making everything an expression of adoration in spirit and truth.

Prayer

*O Jesus Christ, send your Holy Spirit to your
Church, to all of us, that we may put all our
faith and trust in you and be converted to your
Gospel; that we may put it into practice, and be
your messengers and witnesses during all our
lives. Let our highest and most urgent desire be
to spread your Gospel, to make your loving
presence known to all. Give to each of us the
blessing of a community of salvation that helps
us to discover joy, strength of faith, and trust in
you.*

*Let us be rooted, Lord, not in human traditions
alone, but in a community of faith that gives us
the experience of your living presence in this,
our own time in the history of salvation.*

Part Five

Signs
of the
New Law

The Law *of* Grace

Christ has promulgated his law—of grace, of faith, of hope and love, and of adoration in spirit and truth—by his life and death, by his example and words, and, above all, by the outpouring of the grace of the Holy Spirit. All that Christ taught on the Mount of the Beatitudes and on Mount Calvary has effectively touched his disciples only through the Spirit promised to them: *"The Advocate, the Holy Spirit, whom the Father will send in my name, will teach you everything, and remind you of all that I have said to you"* (John 14:26; see also 15:26-27; 16:12-15).

In the sacraments, Christ continues to teach us his law with words and signs, through his Church in its testimony of faith, hope, and adoring love, and principally through the grace of the Holy Spirit. Thus the sacraments are effective signs of *"the law of the Spirit of life in Christ Jesus"* (Romans 8:2a).

The people of the old Covenant saw its sacraments as means and signs for the realization of *ritual purity.* Although the various liturgical celebrations could arouse faith, the dominant perspective in which they had come to be seen was external. We, on the other hand, see sacraments as effective signs of *internal purity.* What the sacraments communicate to followers of Christ is not observance of a written law or a code but, primarily and essentially, a life guided by the Spirit. Through the sacraments, God prompts—in us and through us—a law of charity and justice which characterizes people of the new Covenant. *"Our competence is from God, who has made us competent to be ministers of a new covenant, not of letter but of spirit; for the letter kills, but the Spirit gives life"* (2 Corinthians 3:5b-6).

The new law is characterized by its intimate relation to the new Covenant. This Covenant with the Church, which Christ sealed in his blood on the altar of the cross, is *the great and fundamental sacrament* which is present and operative in a privileged way in the seven sacraments. Therefore, if we want to penetrate the essential character of the new law, we must consider it in the light of the new Covenant and of the sacraments which signify it.

The unity between the interior law, written in the heart, and the exterior law, expressed in formulas, is unfolded in every liturgical celebration. The sacraments are visible signs which manifest interior grace. In them, the signified grace is more important than the sign which signifies it. Nevertheless, we ordinarily do not arrive at interior grace except by means of external and visible signs, that is, by means of the sacraments.

THE AUTHORITY OF SIGNS

The grace of the Holy Spirit infinitely surpasses all that the sacramental signs or words succeed in expressing. The seven sacraments can never monopolize the activity of the Holy Spirit. They can, however, help us to better understand all that the Holy Spirit does, and not only by themselves, but by all signs of the goodness and power of God. Our understanding of the sacraments is normally the result of many experiences and signs of love in our daily lives.

One and undivided is the law of Christ, both internal and external. But its principal part, indeed its *quintessence*, is the grace of the Holy Spirit.

Through faith active in love, all gifts of God enter into the dynamics of grace. The truly graced render thanks to God by using all their talents and goods, as well as their special charism, for the benefit of others: the building up of the Body of Christ. Discerning Christians remember the written law, but know that the law of grace which is engraved in their hearts is richer, stronger, and more gentle than the written law. All criteria of discernment becomes effective through purity of heart: watchfulness about our motives; a trust in God that is acquired through knowledge, experience, and reflection; and the precious wisdom of the Spirit.

Prayer

Each day is a new revelation of your love, O Lord. You multiply the signs of your kindness and goodness. Each day you give us the strength to listen to you, to become more aware of your presence and to respond to you. You have given us ears to hear when you call us through your Word, and through our sisters and brothers.

Each day you open our eyes to see and to admire your works. Each day you allow us to discover signs of your coming, where others hear only noise and see only disaster. Lord, you

are always near to us; you come each day to call
us. You always wait for us. Make us grateful,
make us vigilant.

PARTICIPATION IN CHRIST'S PRIESTHOOD

Through the sacraments, Christ invites us to follow him, just as, in his earthly life, he invited Peter
and James and John. But the instruction the Lord himself gave to his apostles, through words and deeds,
was incomplete before the outpouring of the Holy
Spirit. Similarly, the external invitation which is
extended to us in the sacramental signs would be fruit-
less without the internal grace. The sacraments thus
reveal to us the true nature of the following of Christ.

"He has abolished the law with its command-
ments and ordinances, that he might create
in himself one new humanity in place of the
two, thus making peace, and might reconcile
both groups to God in one body through the
cross, thus putting to death that hostility
through it."

Ephesians 2:15-16

Through the sacraments, Christ makes us participants in his prophetic priesthood and its fruits.

The new law of Christ is a law characterized by
and intimately joined to his priesthood. In the Letter
to the Hebrews, all that is said of the new law written
in the heart is constantly placed in relation to the
priesthood of Christ in its surprising newness. *"Since*
we have confidence to enter the sanctuary by the

blood of Jesus...let us approach with a true heart in full assurance of faith" (Hebrews 10:19,22a).

The heart of the matter is *configuration with Christ*. Its sacramental character is consecration according to the high-priestly prayer of Christ:

> *"Sanctify them in the truth; your word is truth. As you have sent me into the world, so I have sent them into the world. And for their sakes I sanctify myself, so that they also may be sanctified in truth."*

John 17:17-19

In this vision of the sacramental character, ritualism and/or "magic"are excluded. Consecration or ordination is of no avil if it is not oriented to a life totally dedicated to the glory of God and the redemption of humankind in the discipleship of Christ.

Prayer

Here I am, Lord; you have come into my life from the very beginning.You have given me a body and life. You have made me what I am. Here I am, O Lord, to do your will.

Here I am, Lord; send me wherever you want. Make me ready, keep me awake, cleanse my heart even with fire, even by cross and suffering, by difficulties and opposition. Lord, take away from me everything that hinders me from recognizing your coming. Grant everything that leads me closer to you. Lord, here I am, call me; send me.

LIFE IN CHRIST

Faith, and the sacraments of faith, speak of an undeserved gift and vocation that can only be expressed in symbols, images, dim reflections in a mirror (see 1 Corinthians 13:12). Neither rationalism nor moralism will ever understand The Word: *"But to all who received him, who believed in his name, he gave power to become children of God...born...of God"* (John 1:12,13ac). This relationship to Christ is the work of the Holy Spirit, who is grafting our lives on to Christ's. *"No one can enter the kingdom of God without being born of water and Spirit....what is born of the Spirit is spirit"* (John 3:5,6b; see also 1 Peter 1:23).

Above all, the prayers that follow the institution of the Eucharist point to the new life of disciples as life in a mysterious union with Christ's own life, and thus life with the Father. The unity and love between Christ and the Father become the source of our lives, and also the rule for our lives. The triune life of God becomes visible in Christ, who communicates it to us and writes it into our being by the grace of the Holy Spirit.

All that is visible in the sacraments points, not only to the internal relationship with Christ, but also to the pursuit of making this relationship visible in our lives. The sacraments keeps us conscious of the truth that discipleship cannot be reduced to a mere external imitation of Christ. The imitation of Christ follows the sacramental configuration to Christ, but we must not consider so much the single acts of the earthly life of Christ as the mysteries of Christ. We ought to imitate the virtues that Christ reveals in the mysteries of the Incarnation, passion and death, Resurrection and Ascension.

When death came to the last of those who testified from their personal experience with Jesus as the Christ, the author of the fourth gospel pledged himself to show how the historical Jesus, described by the synoptic gospels, was the same as the Christ who was living and operating in the mysteries of the Church. The testimony of John is absolutely valid, even particularly precious, because he grasped the historical truth in greater depth in the light of the mystery of the Church. The Gospel of John centers on the mysteries of the Word Incarnate, his passion, and his Resurrection. By means of baptism and Eucharist, the faithful become participants in the saving death of Christ, and thus unite themselves to the glorious Christ who will come anew. Thus does John intimately combine the words and signs of the earthly Jesus with the sacraments.

Prayer

We ask you, Lord, to give to your Church the experience of a new Pentecost. May all the languages, all the temperaments and charisms of all people unite in a great chorus to your praise. Grant us a community of sisters and brothers who, with their deep faith and prayer, can strengthen our faith where it falls short. Cleanse us, O Lord, and unite us in a joyous faith through which we can comfort the sufferers and support them in their faith.

Come, Holy Spirit, free us from closed minds, from isolation, from anguish and mistrust. Make us free for you, docile to your inspirations, so that all our lives may become one voice, one outcry of joy: "Abba, Father!"